THE GAZE OF MEDUSA

Beautiful Women Who Have Influenced Humanity

Hallman Bonnie

Contents

THE FEMALE GAZE AND MEDUSA

Medusa, the goddess of Greek mythology, has been and continues to be a symbol of feminine power and radiance. Women perceive her as a motivational symbol who encourages them to unleash their beauty in order to gain power despite oppression and adversity. Medusa is a victim of a fate that many ancient and modern women have experienced or may relate with. In ancient Greece, Medusa was a symbol of feminine empowerment, and more recently, for 21st-century women and nonbinary persons. Medusa, with her serpent hair and stone-like look, survives as an allegorical figure of fatal beauty or a convenient image for superimposing the face of a despised woman in power today. In other terms, Medusa is the ultimate femme fatale. She is a lady that embodies a contradictory picture of feminine authority, one that appears appealing on the surface but hides a dangerous or dark underbelly. Medusa's story in general encourages women to get closer to "her sexuality, to her womanly character, allowing her access to her natural strength."

The Gaze of Medusa is a powerful portrayal of women's ambitions and concerns. It reveals women's strength and fragility as they build resistance to hostile living conditions and fixes a panoptic gaze as they learn to deflect humanity's scary glare by fiercely returning their gaze, devising and inventing solutions to hazardous living situations that threaten humanity. Some stare back and win; others are stared down, driven to psychic trauma, psychosis, and even death as a result of this. Because it represents the "image of female intoxication, and seductive attractiveness," the Gaze of Medusa is so alluring to humans. It appeals to us because of its modern applicability and dimensionality. Because it is a symbol of female power in the face of challenged male authority, it retains its historical significance.

In an issue of the Met's quarterly Bulletin on the show, Kiki Karoglou, associate curator in the Department of Greek and Roman Art and organizer of Dangerous Beauty, wrote, "Beauty, like monstrosity, enthralls, and female beauty in particular was perceived and, to a certain extent, is still perceived to be both enchanting and dangerous, or even fatal." Even prominent men couldn't resist her allure because of her attractiveness. She has the ability to be both seductive and harmful, and in some cases, lethal.

Beautiful women who have influenced mankind and the globe at large have demonstrated that being a woman with bodily autonomy and beauty is not at all typical that those should be pushed aside or have authority taken away from them.

Medusa is thus utilized to depict current female politicians, ranging from Angela Merkel to Hillary Clinton (with Trump as Perseus in a popular manifestation). "Over the last fifty years or so, there have been numerous well-publicized feminist initiatives to reclaim The Gaze of Medusa for female power.

HUMANITY'S PROBLEMS THROUGHOUT TIME

There have been several problems that have faced humanity throughout history, which women of various races and colors have battled and won with their feminine force and beauty in order to establish a decent living environment for humanity. Although some of these issues are still prevalent now. Beautiful women have labored and fought to decrease these abnormalities that impact humanity to a minimal and bearable level, by utilizing their female gaze and power to inspire change and a good reversal to these issues.

The following are some of the challenges that has faced humanity through time:

Inequality Between Men And Women

One of the most important parts of gender inequality around the world was the right to vote and how women were restricted or prevented from voting. The ability to contribute to the choice of a government that will represent your ideas is a fundamental right. Given that the government has the capacity to make decisions that affect individuals' everyday lives, it is critical that those who are affected have a say in who makes those decisions; unfortunately, this was not the case, as women were excluded from voting. Women were not granted voting rights until much later, and only after a series of hard fought fights. The suffrage campaign, led by Emmeline Pankhurst, who created the Women's Social and Political Union (WSPU) in 1903, strived to attain women's equality by peaceful and legal means such as petitions, albeit the movement was more militant in its actions. This group attempted to enter parliament, heckled members of parliament, damaged and shackled themselves to property, and as a result, received media hatred and were physically assaulted by police, prompting women to vote. Another historical issue to gender inequity was female restrictions on educational needs. Girls were more likely to get a home education geared toward their future responsibilities as wives and mothers, or to be rewarded for a variety of accomplishments, such as learning to play the piano. Mathematics and science were traditionally designated for boys who were expected to pursue a career path. Women are more likely to pursue Social Sciences and Humanities disciplines and are underrepresented in Science, Technology, Engineering, and Mathematics even after these limits were lifted and eliminated. There are still individuals who believe that women are unsuitable for careers in science.

Society Of The Absolute Partriach

Another type of gender inequality was the Absolute Patriarchal Society. There was an expression of masculine social power and privilege, but no developmental path toward equality, peace, and prosperity was taken. Women fell under the protection of their husbands and became one person in the eyes of the law when they married, giving them no rights to possess property or keep their earnings, which became their husband's property. Even though the wife possessed riches previous to marriage, it became the husband's property when the couple married. Although limits on property ownership were in place in England and Wales until the 1870 Married Woman's Property Act.

Government Of Dictatorship

Several dictatorships have risen throughout history. Several socialist regimes were overthrown during the Cold War, leading to brutal dictatorships and tyranny in various countries. For example, the period known as El Salvador's Military Dictatorship began in 1931, according to Civic Directory. Several crimes against humanity were committed by this dictatorship, including La Matanza. Rafael Leónidas Trujillo ruled the Dominican Republic from 1942 until 1952, persecuting Communists and their opponents. The Parsley massacre occurred, with the main goal of assassinating Haitian immigrants living in the Dominican Republic. It is estimated that 12,168 people were killed, including President Élie Lescot of Haiti, 12,136 people killed and 2419 injured by Jean Price-Mars, 17,000 people killed by Joaquin Balaguer, and 35,000 killed by Bernardo Vega. When Trujillo was assassinated in the city of Santo Domingo in 1961, the dictatorship in the Dominican Republic came to an end.

This book, on the other hand, introduces powerful and beautiful women throughout history who raised standards, overcoming the hurdles mentioned above and more by seizing power via their beauty and sexuality, allowing them to positively influence humanity.

MEDUSA'S HISTORICAL BACKGROUND

Medusa was one of Gorgon's sisters born by the primordial sea gods Keto and Phorkys; Medusa and her sisters were nurtured on the island of Sarpedon by Phorkys and Keto. Medusa was mortal, while the others, Sthenno the strong and Euryale the far springer, were immortal; their father was a sea deity, and Ceto, her mother, was a sea monster goddess. All three gorgons were born to Ceto: Sthenno, Euryale, and Medusa. The only Gorgon who was mortal was Medusa, whereas the other two were immortal. Echidna and Ladon, two of Phorkys and Ceto's three Gorgon's daughters, are awful and fearsome monsters. Medusa was a beautiful maiden who was exceedingly gentle and devout until she aroused the wrath of Athena, who transformed Medusa into a ferocious monster with snakes for hair owing to an ill-fated love affair with Poseidon.

Medusa was a stunning young woman who served as a priestess to Athena, the goddess of wisdom and war. Medusa was an excellent priestess, swearing to the goddess that she would live a life of celibacy and servitude. Medusa was a devoted woman who spent her youth learning to become a priestess of a goddess she adored and thought to be the most powerful of all the Olympians. Medusa was also a favorite of Athena since she was a gorgeous woman who chose the goddess over any male. Medusa vowed to remain a virgin while serving Athena, one of only three virgin goddesses. Medusa's hair was one of her most attractive features, drawing people to her. On the other hand, notwithstanding her stunning beauty, Medusa vowed celibacy.

Both mortals and gods would recognize Medusa's beauty while serving Athena. Medusa did not partake in any of the attention she received until Poseidon, the god of the oceans and competitor of Athena, saw Medusa and was enamored. Still, Medusa did not pay notice because she had pledged to remain a virgin. Poseidon, however, noticed Medusa one day and decided to dishonor Athena by rapping the priestess on the temple steps. Poseidon then fled, leaving Medusa vulnerable and helpless.

Medusa appealed to Athena for forgiveness and direction. Since the gods claimed their lovers as their partners for all eternity in those days, Medusa was now Poseidon's wife.

The eternal rivalry between Athena and Poseidon, on the other hand, affects much more than just those two; it divides Olympus and destroys many lives.

In Greek mythology, gods acted in irrational, petty ways, and the goddess of wisdom was no exception. Hence, she cursed Medusa for breaking her promise of celibacy by casting a horrible curse on her.

Medusa's gorgeous locks turned into venomous snakes, and anybody who stared into Medusa's eyes turned to stone. Medusa's hair grew into a snake nest that rattled around her head. This incident transformed Medusa's kind, virtuous personality into one that fit her new look due to these traumatic experiences.

Medusa was a dreaded creature among the Greeks, a monster whose terrifying gaze turns onlookers and anybody who dares to look into her eyes into stone. When Athena turned Medusa into a monster, she gained immense power: the ability to turn humans into stone and to freeze and stop time.

The ability to kill someone with a single glance is terrifying, and it can be exploited to inflict havoc. She, however, dwell on the island, cut off from everyone but her sisters and those who came to kill her. Perseus, a man, charged by another man, Polydectes, to kill Medusa, defeated her.

Her story does not end there; even though she was dead, her power remained, as Medusa's severed head became a symbol that frightened away evil after Perseus slaughtered her.

Many warriors wore the Medusa's head insignia on their shields and breastplates to help them win during the battle. Medusa's logo appears on ancient Greek coins, which are now old antiques, and assists in battle.

Even though everyone despised Medusa, she remained a significant element of Greek culture and a key symbol. Medusa appears in various mythical myths, and she is also shown in a variety of forms in ancient art. Her look changes dramatically over time, yet her stunning frontality instantly recognizes her.

A figure facing directly out is uncommon in Greek art, yet Medusa, regardless of style or medium, stares straight forward and uncompromisingly confront the observer in practically every rendition.

THE EFFECT OF MEDUSA'S GAZE AND THE MEDUSA MYTH

Looking straight into Medusa's eyes, according to Greek mythology, would turn a person to stone. After she was cursed, she became a historical threat.

Medusa was a winged Gorgon creature with snakes for hair who had the power to turn people to stone simply by looking into their eyes. Though a product of Athena's curse and punishment, Medusa's gaze became a weapon and a source of strength for her.

Medusa was pursued by powerful masculine figures, Kings, and gods who perceived her gaze and everything she possessed as a threat to them. Because of the terrifying power of her gaze, Medusa became a hunted cursed victim.

Medusa's gaze symbolized power and the capacity to slay one's foes. She was regarded as a formidable opponent.

Her head is a protective symbol, and it was even adopted as a symbol of French emancipation and freedom during the French Revolution. The most well-known story recounts her fateful encounter with the Greek hero Perseus.

According to legend, King Polydectes requested gifts to be presented to him in honor of the king's marriage to Perseus' mother, Danae. However, because Perseus could not present a gift, King Polydectes commanded him to bring him the specific gift of Medusa's head.

This declaration was stated by King Polydectes to dismiss and dissuade Perseus, as the mission for Medusa's head was believed unattainable.

On the other hand, Perseus accepted the challenge and headed off to fetch Medusa's head for the king.

Perseus sets off on a journey to find and decapitate Medusa. The gods provide him gifts to help him defeat her, including a shield created by Athena, the goddess of knowledge and wisdom. Without this shield, Perseus would not have been able to complete his conquest. Perseus got the assistance of Athena and Hermes and persuaded the Graeae to reveal Medusa's location and dwelling place.

Perseus arrived in the famous country of the Gorgons, located far west, beyond the outer Ocean, with the rocky island of Sarpedon in the middle. He cut off her head with his sickle and carried it back to King Polydectes in his sack.

While the Gorgons were sleeping, Perseus attacked, using Athena's polished shield to see Medusa's hideous visage. He used Athena's bronze shield as a guide to avoiding gazing directly at the Gorgons and being turned to stone; he decapitated her with a harpe, an adamantine sword.

Medusa's children, Chrysaor, the golden giant, and Pegasus, the famed white-winged horse who emerged from her neck and blood, were born due to such a horrific event.

The Gorgons were startled by the uproar and tried their hardest to avenge her sister's death, but they couldn't see or capture Perseus because he was wearing Hades' Invisibility Cap and Hermes' winged shoes. As a result, they returned to their remote hideaway to mourn Medusa. Perseus used the head to turn his adversaries to stone and save the princess Andromeda from a sea monster during his travels.

Hearing Gordon's sister's sad and enraged cries, Athena was inspired to create the flute to imitate them. When the goddess played the flute, she threw it away after catching a glimpse of herself in the mirror; her face bloated and turned ugly as she played. While she successfully replicated the Gorgons' wails, she unintentionally resembled their vast and frightening looks.

On the other hand, death could not stop Medusa, so Perseus had to preserve her decapitated head in a special sack called a kybisis. He used the head to turn his opponents to stone and save Princess Andromeda from a sea monster before delivering it to Athena for her aegis.

Perseus turned Medusa's head and gaze against King Polydectes by turning him to stone upon his return, which was ironic. Perseus took Medusa's head from his pouch and held it up, leading King Polydectes to look into Medusa's eyes and be turned to stone.

Perseus then delivered Medusa's head to Athena, his benefactor, as a votive gift. He placed it under Zeus' aegis, which she also wore as the gorgoneion. She collected some of the remaining blood and delivered the majority to Asclepius, who used Medusa's left side to kill people and the blood from her right side to revive the dead. Athena handed the rest of Medusa's blood to her adoptive son, Erichthonius, in a bottle containing two droplets of blood, one of which was a cure-all and the other a lethal poison, according to Euripides.

Like the modern evil eye, Medusa became an emblem of protection and warding off the negative. She was a lethal threat meant to discourage other murderous threats, a picture of evil meant to repel evil. Thanks to her snake hair and stone-like glare, Medusa became a symbol of deadly beauty and a convenient image for superimposing the face of a despised woman in authority. Perseus, her slayer, is shown with a severed head, an image with its name, the gorgoneion, sculpted, painted, or carved and held aloft by her.

Perseus, her slayer, is shown with a severed head, an image with its name, the gorgoneion, sculpted, painted, or carved and held aloft by her.

Medusa's head and face were and still are used as a "gorgoneion," a popular decorative motif in ancient Greece. It's a familiar emblem of her power found in architecture, vase painting, and metalwork. During the Archaic period, the gorgoneion was a common motif in temple decoration.

MARGARET THATCHER

BACKGROUND

Margaret Thatcher's full name is Margaret Hilda Roberts, Baroness Thatcher of Kesteven, née Margaret Hilda Thatcher, was born in Grantham, Lincolnshire, England, on October 13, 1925; tiny town in the English county of Lincolnshire She passed away in April of 2013.

Alfred and Beatrice, her parents, were ardent Methodists and middle-class shopkeepers. Alfred was also a politician, having served on the Grantham Town Council for ten years before becoming an alderman in 1943 and mayor from 1945 to 1946. Her father was a respected town leader who served as a lay leader in their church, a local councilor, and eventually as mayor.

He told Margaret that she should never do things just because others are doing them; instead, she should do what she believes is right and persuade others to join her. Margaret thus grew up with a strong desire to lead and positively impact humanity. Muriel was her older sister, but she had no brothers or close relatives.

Margaret was born in a community still recovering from the Great War, which lasted from 1914 to 1918. As she grew older, people began to worry that another conflict would erupt, and this was, regrettably, their fate. Margaret was 14 years old when World War II began in 1939 and lasted until 1945 when she was 20 years old. Many folks had no work and very little money when they were growing up.

The Roberts family had better luck, and they baked for individuals who were sick or didn't have enough to eat, which their church members distributed. Every Sunday, they attended church together. So Margaret Thatcher grew up in a world when awful things were happening, and life was more complicated than it is now.

Even amidst all of this, people assisted one another and were proud of their town and country. Margaret's basic orientation led to her aura's ability to impact humanity for the better.

She went to public schools and worked hard, eventually earning a seat at Oxford University to study chemistry, a subject she liked when she was 18 years old. Her Oxford professor was a well-known chemist who went on to win the Nobel Prize for her work.

Her father was always concerned about happenings and was involved in their local council administration. He taught her a lot, and she appreciated listening to him explain how things worked; this inspired and contributed to her plans to pursue politics. She began volunteering when she was eleven years old during an election.

She studied chemistry at Oxford University from 1943 to 1947, but it was evident that politics was her genuine calling. Thatcher has wanted to be a politician since she was a child.

Her passion drove her to Oxford University, where she studied chemistry and became involved in politics almost immediately. Becoming one of the first female presidents of the Oxford University Conservative Association, this was a small election. Still, some well-known politicians spoke to her group, and she developed a valuable network and relationships that would later benefit her.

She worked as a research chemist for four years after graduating in 1947, reading for the bar in her spare time. She worked as a barrister, specializing in tax law in 1954.

Denis Thatcher, a wealthy industrialist who backed her political ambitions, married her in December 1951. Mark Thatcher and Carol Thatcher were the couple's twins, a boy, and a daughter. She was studying for the bar exams simultaneously, which she passed in early 1954.

She spent the next few years practicing law and looking for a viable political constituency. She worked as a tax lawyer in the 1950s before being elected to Parliament from Finchley in 1959.

In 1950, she ran for parliament in Dartford, Kent, a Labour-dominated constituency, with "Vote Right to Keep What's Left." The Labour Party defeated her in both that year and 1951, but she earned more votes than previous Conservative Party candidates. In 1951, she tried one more. She didn't have a chance because most Dartford voters supported the Labour Party. She was, however, the country's youngest female candidate, and she was beautiful. Thus her photo appeared in numerous newspapers. She had a great time campaigning for the elections.

She was later elected to the cabinet as Minister of Pensions several years later. In 1970, she got appointed as the Minister of Education, garnering the nickname "Thatcher, the Milk Snatcher" for eliminating free milk from schools as part of a budget-cutting program.

After the Conservative Party lost both national elections in 1974, she defeated Edward Heath for the Conservative Party leadership.

Thatcher was Europe's first female prime minister. She accelerated the British economy from statism to liberalism and became, by personality as much as achievement, the most renowned British political leader since Winston Churchill. Thatcher was the only Prime Minister to win three terms consecutively in the twentieth century and, at the time of her resignation, Britain's longest continuously serving prime minister since 1827.

Thatcher ran for Parliament for the first time in 1950 but lost despite boosting the local Conservative vote by 50%. She was appointed to the House of Commons in 1959 and won the "safe" Conservative seat of Finchley in northern London.

She steadily ascended through the ranks of the Conservative Party, serving as a parliamentary secretary in the Ministry of Pensions and National Insurance in 1961, chief opposition spokeswoman on education in 1969, and secretary of state for education and science in the Edward Heath government in 1970.

Thatcher was the second woman to hold a cabinet ministry in a Conservative government; she abolished a program that offered free milk to students, causing a storm of controversy and prompted Labour Party opponents to ridicule her with chants of "Thatcher, the milk snatcher."

She also established more comprehensive schools than any other education minister in history, even though they undermined them during her tenure as Prime Minister. The

Labour Party introduced Comprehensive schools in the 1960s to provide rigorous academic education to working-class children.

After Heath lost two consecutive elections in 1974, Thatcher was the only minister willing to challenge him for the party leadership, despite her low position in the party hierarchy.

She was appointed as the leader of the Conservative Party in February 1975, with the support of the Conservative right-wing. She thus started a 15-year tenure that transformed the face of British politics. Thatcher remained a prominent political force after 1990.

She toured the world for 12 years speaking and authored two best-selling memoirs, "The Downing Street Years" in 1993 and "The Path to Power" in 1995.

In March 2002, she was leaving public speaking due to medical advice. In her later years, her health deteriorated, and she grew increasingly forgetful. However, she continued to enjoy life and had many friends and admirers.

In a lavish ceremony, Margaret died in April 2013 got buried at St Paul's Cathedral. The Queens, the Prime Minister, and other notables from worldwide were in attendance. Soldiers from the Welsh Guards carried her coffin, a regiment that had fought bravely in the Falklands War.

MODERN BRITISH POLITICS GETTING A NEW LOOK

Between 1979 and 1990, Margaret Thatcher served as Prime Minister of the United Kingdom for over 12 years. She was the first woman to hold that position or govern any significant country in Europe or America, and she became well-known worldwide. Many Britain questioned whether a woman could handle such a challenging job when she became Prime Minister.

She demonstrated that the answer to that question was a resounding 'yes.' Whenever a woman became the head of a country, she was frequently compared to Margaret Thatcher, even though they were very different.

Margaret Thatcher entered a competition among Members of Parliament shortly after her election to earn the chance to pass a bill. She won the first time and had her law written and met significant individuals in Parliament and impressing other Members of Parliament with her "maiden speech."

The next day, she conducted her first-ever television interview, sitting on the couch with the twins on either side of her. Soon after, she got propositioned to join the government as a member in charge of pensions and benefits.

Margaret studied hard and was skilled at grasping all the intricate rules. She became well-known, and when Edward Heath became Prime Minister in 1970, she was appointed Education Secretary, with responsibility for Britain's schools and institutions.

She terminated a program that offered free milk to students while in the Heath administration, causing a storm of controversy and prompting Labour Party opponents to mock her as "Thatcher, the milk snatcher."

She also established additional, comprehensive schools, which the Labour Party selected to provide academic education to working-class students. After Heath lost two consecutive elections in 1974, Thatcher was the only minister willing to challenge him for the party leadership, despite his low position in the party hierarchy. She was elected leader in February 1975, with the support of the Conservative right-wing, and thus started a 15-year reign that would reshape the face of Britain.

Following a series of strikes during the "Winter of Discontent" under James Callaghan's government, Thatcher led the Conservatives to a landslide electoral victory in 1979.

As Prime Minister of the Conservative Party, Thatcher advocated for individual independence from the state, including privatization of state-owned enterprises; the sale of public housing to tenants. She also effected cuts in social spending such as health care, education, and housing; limitations on printing money following the monetarism economic doctrine; and legal restrictions on trade unions. This action gave rise to the term "Thatcherism," which came to refer not only to these policies but also to certain aspects of her ethics and personal styles, such as moral absolutism, fierce nationalism, a concern for individual interests, and an unyielding approach to achieving political goals.

One of the most critical contributions Thatcher made to development was transformative leadership. She changed the course of her country and the understanding of what a UK prime minister can do and how.

She played a role in the fall of the Berlin Wall, which marked the beginning of a significant shift in central and eastern European economies from reliance on central planning to market-based governance.

Due to large budget deficits and a falling pound, the previous Labour Party had to seek an emergency loan from the International Monetary Fund. Mrs. Thatcher, an English patriot from the Elgar and Churchill schools, saw the decision as a national humiliation.

And as part of her commitment to reduce inflation and balance the budget, Margaret Thatcher's government cut spending. When the inevitable recession hit, she resisted calls for a change of strategy, telling the Conservative Party Conference in 1981, "The lady's not turning." With her emphasis on boosting competitiveness and labor and product market flexibility, Thatcher affected Britain's economic policy.

Her emphasis on market deregulation continues to impact much of the work of the Organization for Economic Cooperation and Development (OECD).

Thatcher was a firm believer in privatization's benefits. Her admirers credit her for helping the British economy recover. In 1980 and 1990, these policies were at the center of the IMF and World Bank's structural adjustment initiatives for developing nations.

In previous decades, when significant parties were in power, there seemed to be an endless succession of labor strikes that brought Britain to a halt. Margaret Thatcher's deconstruction of the British trade union movement's industrial power led to the birth of an economic revolution.

The previous regime wasted millions of days a year due to strike action in the late 1970s. At the end of Thatcher's tenure, the number of days lost was a fraction of what had been. The unions' strike weapons gradually emasculated.

Margaret Thatcher's governments initiated several measures carried out by subsequent administrations and were traceable to the Thatcher years. Ken Baker developed grant-maintained schools and city technical colleges, which were the forerunners of academies, first introduced by Labour and later expanded by Michael Gove.

She had policy goals when she became Prime Minister, and she dealt with education policy because it was her comfort zone in terms of public services. She has previously served as the Secretary of Education. Margaret Thatcher is still a hot topic of debate. Many of her policies, according to critics, were overly harsh and damaged individuals.

On the other hand, Defenders claim that she improved the British economy and improved most people's lives. However, both detractors and supporters believe that Margaret Thatcher's tenure as prime minister significantly impacted British politics.

THE IRON LADY OF POLITICS

Margaret Thatcher was named and tagged the "Iron Lady" by a Soviet journalist, a moniker linked with her uncompromising policies and leadership style.

In May 1979, she was elected Prime Minister and served for eleven and a half years, the longest British prime minister's tenure in the twentieth century. She was a committed capitalist as Prime Minister, determined to wipe socialism from the face of the United Kingdom.

She slashed direct taxes, spending, and regulations, privatized state industries and housing, overhauled the education, health, and welfare systems, and promoted traditional values during her term.

Several challenges filled her term in government, including an economic downturn, inner-city rioting, and a miners' strike.

The Falklands War of 1982 was Thatcher's first victory as Prime Minister when she dispatched British troops to recapture British holdings off the coast of South America seized and controlled by Argentina. The British won the war, proving that the United Kingdom was a force to be respected once again.

During her presidency, the middle and upper classes experienced unparalleled economic prosperity, but this was offset by unemployment levels not seen since the 1930s, an increase in homelessness, and the demise of Britain's major industries.

She was a fervent supporter of Ronald Reagan, the Republican president of the United States. They both backed stringent foreign and defense policies, but they also built a positive relationship with reformist Soviet leader Mikhail Gorbachev, which contributed to the end of the Cold War.

After Saddam Hussein invaded Kuwait in 1990, Thatcher encouraged President George Bush to send troops to Saudi Arabia. Her unyielding support for the Poll Tax and refusal to adopt a unified currency for Europe led to a brutal internal rebellion within the Conservative Party, which forced her out of office.

In November 1990, she had to quit as Prime Minister. Since leaving office, Baroness Thatcher in the House of Lords was the name they called her.

She lectured worldwide, supporting her beliefs, and she was the president of several organizations dedicated to her interests. Her health had deteriorated, so she had stopped speaking in public.

She is known as the United Kingdom's first female Prime Minister and served from 1979 until 1990. During her time in office, she limited the influence of trade unions, privatized some industries, decreased public benefits, and modified the rules of political discourse, much like her friend and ideological partner, US President Ronald Reagan.

Because she fought Soviet communism and fought to maintain the Falkland Islands under British sovereignty, she got tagged the "Iron Lady."

Thatcher, the longest-serving prime minister in history, was forced to resign by her own Conservative Party members.

In 2007, Margaret Thatcher became the first living British ex-prime minister to be honored with a statue in the Houses of Parliament. It's next to a statue of Winston Churchill in the lobby of the House of Commons.

Margaret Thatcher's second term in office began with nearly as many challenges as her first. From 1984 to 1985, the miners' union called a year-long strike.

After a long and difficult battle, she defeated the union, and many of MT's opponents in the Labour Party began to believe that she could not change things.

The Irish Republican Army attempted to murder Margaret Thatcher and many of her colleagues by bombing their hotel in Brighton during the Conservative Party annual conference in October 1984, while the strike was still ongoing. Even though she was unharmed, some of her closest friends were hurt or killed.

The attackers came dangerously close to killing her because the attack heavily destroyed the room next to her bedroom. She refused to be intimidated by terrorism and opposed it in all of its forms.

She persisted in completing the Conservative Convention the next day after the Irish Republican Army attempted to assassinate her and her Cabinet at the 1984 Conservative Convention in Brighton, nearly missing Thatcher but killing five others. This attack demonstrated how tough a leader she was.

Some Conservatives have always been wary of Margaret Thatcher as the party's leader. One of these opponents, Minister of defense Michael Heseltine, abruptly quit in January 1986, walking out of a meeting at No.10 Downing Street over the problems of the British helicopter manufacturer Westland.

Margaret Thatcher not only survived the crisis, but she emerged unscathed. There was chatter that the administration and its leader were 'weary,' that they had gone on for far too long. Margaret's response to the critics was typical: she declared her intention to form a third Thatcher government!

With the economy in such good shape, the chances of an election were favorable, and the administration got re-elected.

She was now a well-known international figure, particularly close to Ronald Reagan, the US President. They were both harsh critics of the Soviet Union's communist policies, which had been at odds with Western Europe and the United States since the late 1940s.

People referred to the "Cold War" as a conflict where there was no direct fighting between the powers, but there was plenty of tension and menace.